Highest Net Profit Form▪▪▪

The Zero Bullshit Guide to Selling Your
Home For The Highest Net Profit in a
Timeframe You Control With An Agent
That Delivers Results...

ZERO BS ESTATE AGENCY

2

JOHN SAVAGE

COPYRIGHT

JOHN SAVAGE

TABLE OF CONTENTS

COPYRIGHT *4*

71,228% RETURN ON A £7 INVESTMENT *10*

WHY I WROTE THIS BOOK *16*

FORWARD *20*

WHAT YOU HAVE IN YOUR HANDS *24*

INTRODUCTION *26*

THE RULES [TRUTHS] OF THE GAME *32*

"QUICK STORY..." *34*

"MY PROMISE TO YOU..." *40*

"HOW TO USE THIS BOOK..." *43*

STEP 1 - "6 MONTHS, 1 MILE..." *46*

STEP 2 - "CHECK AGENT STATS..." *48*

STEP 3 - "ASK THE RIGHT QUESTIONS..." *50*

SECRET INSIDER QUESTION #1 .... *53*

SECRET INSIDER QUESTION #2 .... *55*

SECRET INSIDER QUESTION #3 .... *57*

SECRET INSIDER QUESTION #4 .... *59*

SECRET INSIDER QUESTION #5 .... *62*

SECRET INSIDER QUESTION #6 .... *64*

SECRET INSIDER QUESTION #7 .... *67*

SECRET INSIDER QUESTION #8 71

SECRET INSIDER QUESTION #9 73

SECRET INSIDER QUESTION #10............. 76

SECRET INSIDER QUESTION #11................ 79

SECRET INSIDER QUESTION #12................ 85

SECRET INSIDER QUESTION #13................ 87

SECRET INSIDER QUESTION #14................ 89

SECRET INSIDER QUESTION #15................ 91

SECRET INSIDER QUESTION #16................ 95

SECRET INSIDER QUESTION #17................ 96

SECRET INSIDER QUESTION #18................ 98

SECRET INSIDER QUESTION #19................ 101

SECRET INSIDER QUESTION #20................ 104

SECRET INSIDER QUESTION #21................ 106

STEP 4 - "PROPERTY INFORMATION..." 108

STEP 5 - "HOW TO CHOOSE THE RIGHT AGENT..." ... 111

STEP 6 - "BUYER SELLER RELATIONSHIP..." 118

STEP 7 - "AVOID STARS IN YOUR EYE'S VALUATIONS AT ALL COSTS. HERE'S WHY..." 121

STEP 8 - "BUYERS DON'T WANT CHEAP. BUYERS WANT BARGAINS..." 125

STEP 9 - "AT THE END OF THE SALE, ALL THAT MATTERS IS YOUR PROFIT..." 129

"FINAL THOUGHTS...".. *134*

"WHAT NEXT...?" *136*

JOHN SAVAGE

71,228% RETURN ON A £7 INVESTMENT

"I've watched your content on TikTok which lead me to read your e-book...

I took on your advice and tips to get things in place correctly from the beginning.

I met with multiple local agents, after doing some due diligence online first, including the GetAgent data showing their stats.

The first two agents valued the property very similarly... The third quoted £25k higher and insisted he had a buyer lined up who would pay that much. (Spoiler alert, their buyer never materialised).

To be honest, I simply didn't believe him and his comparable evidence didn't stack up to justify a valuation that high.

I went with an agent who had a clear plan for marketing. The little extras like evidence of high-quality photos and a 3D map of the property showed me they were serious about doing the job properly, not looking to save a few quid on the marketing budget, even though they clearly already had a few buyers in mind.

We appointed the agent on the 8th December and photos were arranged for following Wednesday (more to do with my availability than the agent!).

The property was put on the market on the Thursday. 7 viewings arranged back to back for Saturday.

We received 5 offers, 3 of which were at or in excess of the asking price. Accepted an offer in excess of asking price on the Monday.

Of course, there is still plenty of work still to be done but the marketing and agreement on price was almost effortless on my part, due to the preparation upfront..." – Michael Hamilton

- 100% of the buyers showed up to view his home.
- 78% of the buyers offered on his property.
- and 50% that offered were at or the above market value!
- This seller achieved £5,000 more than market value.

- Which meant, an investment of just £7 (at the time) in this book resulted 71,228% Return on Investment.

Let that sink in…

Thing is, when selling your home, the most important thing in the world is achieving the HIGHEST NET PROFIT in timeframe you in **control without the worry of your buyer pulling out.**

Being in control of the sale of your home requires you to be strategic.

And if you're strategic, you'll reap the biggest rewards and leave other sellers (your competition other properties currently being marketed similar to your home) sitting stagnant on the market.

And herein lays a key distinction you've got to be open to. To predictably and properly achieve the highest net profit for your home without stress is understanding this.—>

"THERE'S A VERY BIG DIFFERENCE BETWEEN AN AGENT THAT SAYS THINGS THAT SOUND NICE AND A BLACK BELT AGENT THAT DELIVERS RESULTS..."

Said differently...

There are 2 types of agent.

The **'INTERESTED IN.'**

Ie. Agents interested in winning your instruction (at any cost) for their own gain and then there are agents that are **'EXPERT IN...'**

EXPERT IN agents are in the business of selling houses. Not selling long and unfair sole agency contracts.

They know exactly how to maximise the value of their client's home's.

The **'EXPERT IN'** and **'INTERESTED IN'** are polar opposites.

- The **'INTEREST IN'** agent sells snake oil and elixirs.

- The **'EXPERT IN'** agent consistently produces superior results.
- **'INTERESTED IN'** (amateur agents) are only 'interested in' winning for themselves. Not you. The **'EXPERT AGENT'** is only interested in winning for you.
- Most agents when you first mett them (to your face at least), act like they're your best friend, but behind closed doors, they're not...
- You are just a number. A route to money. A literal KPI.
- According to Rightmove, 60% of sellers sell through the second agent!

In other words, 60% of sellers lost their right to choose what the next chapter in their life looked like.

The moment their property hit the market without those seller's being aware they'd been deliberately trapped in a sinking ship they were get out of...

WHY I WROTE THIS BOOK

The whole purpose of this book is to give you the freedom you deserve when you come to sell your home…

And if you don't want to lose your freedom to choose the outcome of the next chapter of your life, you're going to have to give yourself an advantage...

Trust me on this…

Picking an agent based on the highest valuation (which thousands of homeowners do) means you're happy and willing to vote for the wolf in sheep's clothing.

When done right, selling property is the easiest thing in the world.

But the biggest reason why homeowners fail to achieve the rewards that are rightfully theirs, is because they don't know how to unearth professional agents.

Fact is, unethical agents know they shouldn't make their seller's home look meek and impotent.

But most agents don't have the moral fibre or the courage to tell you the truth.

They know the truth.

But equally, snake oil salesman aren't stupid.

They know truth carries consequences.

The truth carries with it accountability.

The truth forces agents to give professional advice that has accountability attached to it.

So many sellers fall victim to "Star in Your Eye's Valuations…" only to realise their agent was using unethical tactics to win their business…

And by the time they've realised, the damage is done leaving them with a house exposed to an unexcited audience that wouldn't come if you paid them...

I don't want to be so blunt, but these are the facts.

So before you sign a contract or agree to give an agent the keys to your home, you've got to find the agent that has changed the rules of the game in your favour...

So how do you discover the agent that will give your property an advantage over other similar properties that you're competing with in your area?

Follow the 9 steps in this book...

You'll discover how to find the agents that have the talent, knowledge, experience including the skillset to predictably and profitably sell your home for the highest net profit without the anxiety of a traditional, **"whack it on the market strategy..."**

- STEP 1 --> You'll discover the Importance of Adopting a Surveyor's Mindset Before Marketing Your Property"

- STEP 2 --> Expert Tips on Identifying Trustworthy Agents and Weeding Out the Unreliable Ones...

- STEP 3 --> 21 Questions That Will Unlock the Secret to Achieving The Highest Net Profit...

- STEP 4 --> Why Instructing a Solicitor Before Going to Market is Crucial...

- STEP 5 --> How to Distinguish Agents with Genuine Plans from Those Who Rely on Deception

- STEP 6 --> The Most Critical Relationship in the Selling Process...

- STEP 7 --> Why Choosing a Cheap Fee Agent Can Cost You More Than Paying a 2% agent...

- STEP 8 --> How To Generate More Than Market Value For Your Home...

- STEP 9 --> The Characteristics of the 4 Best Types of Buyers"

FORWARD

Circa 2007, I had a buyer on the phone who wouldn't give me her name.

In fact, she wouldn't let me get a word in edgeways.

And when I did manage to get a question in, she point-blank ignored it.

Instead, she half asked but 100% demanded in poignant Scottish accent, "Are you going to show us this property or what!?" I had nothing else in the diary and the property was only a short walk around the corner...

So I said, "Yeah, I'll come."

As I walked, I could see the lady waiting outside the property. Her arms were folded. Her body language angry...

Internally though, I was smiling knowing I was potentially about to make her explode.

I wasn't gonna be a dick.

But I had to do what was right...

So I held out my hand. She left me hanging!

And as she did so, I noticed a man just beyond her right shoulder resting on the side of a parked car...

He looked pissed too!

"This is my husband." She said, immediately followed by, "Are you going to show us this flat or what!?" gesturing with her eyes that I unlock the gate...

Looking directly at her. I held the keys in the hand she didn't shake and politely said, "These are the keys to this flat." Pointing but without looking to where her eyes tried to lead me moments before..

"But unless I know exactly what you're looking for, I can't show you this property."

As expected, she lost it!

"YOU CAN'T SAY THAT! YOU'RE 'JUST' AN ESTATE AGENT..!"

I wasn't mucking around either.

Realising I'd happily walk back to the office without giving it a second thought, she reluctantly told me what their ideal property looked like...

My response was straight and to the point.

"This flat isn't for you." and asked if I could explain why.

To make my point real. I invited them in to the flat to prove I wasn't playing a game.

Back out on the street.

She turned to me and said...

"YOU ARE THE FIRST ESTATE AGENT TO HAVE EVER TOLD US THE TRUTH..!"

Which was when I revealed I had the perfect property for them.

The following Monday, my colleague (who did the viewing for me) slapped me in the face with a full asking price offer...

"Not only that..." he said, "In order to buy, they need to sell…"

"Okay…" I said

"But they'll only agree to instruct us if 'YOU' (as in me, John Savage) COULD SELL IT... No one else!"

The best part.

Neither property sold for a single pound less than their asking price...

WHAT YOU HAVE IN YOUR HANDS

What you have in your hands right now (if actioned) will show exactly who the charlatans are vs the Pro's

In the story above, I didn't do anything special. Selling these properties happened by design. Not a random chance or sold for maximum due to lucky breaks.

I simply followed my process → The Highest Net Profit Formula.

And at the time of writing this book, over the last 43 properties I've sold, I've achieved an average 99.47% valuation accuracy rate (i.e. what I told a seller their property was worth vs what I sold them for) which was well before the market went crazy.

and at that time, compare 99.47% against my local competition valuation accuracy rate of 94%

That's a difference of £18,000 lost on a £300,000 property and yet you'd still owe my competition a fee..?

24

JOHN SAVAGE

INTRODUCTION

In addition to the 'EXPERT IN' and 'INTERESTED IN'', there are three types of Estate Agent.

Professional, Unethical and the 'Dishonourable.

The 'Dishonourables' are agents that lack courage to do what's right because they're more worried about keeping their job than telling sellers the truth... They lack the skill to mould and shape the perfect sale for their clients.

No courage. No guts. They rely on the 'anchoring effect' to sell houses.

Worse, these people take zero responsibility for their actions.

They're literally glorified door openers too scared to tell you what they really think just in case they miss out on winning your instruction.

Keeping their office doors open is more important than doing what's right.

Their priority is selling lengthy contracts, not houses.

And once they've got a seller tied in to a contract, they drift off, leaving sellers to fend for themselves which cost's homeowners thousands of pounds in lost revenue on the real value of their home...

These agents are skilled in the art of bulls*t but massively unskilled in the art of selling property. They don't need talent or the resourcefulness to deliver everything they said they would.

Sellers are trapped and this type of agent holds the keys…

Further, if they end up agreeing a sale, the process from offer being accepted to echanging contracts will be a painful process.

The Unethicals
The 'Unethicals' on the other hand, know exactly what they're doing!

They understand exactly how to take advantage of you...

They understand the allure of 'stars in your eyes' valuations…

They perfected it…

They know how hard it is for sellers to resist the temptation of a huge valuation.

Make no mistake. These guys are skilled. Very skilled. They are incredible salesmen in the art of bullsh*tting making it look sincere, honest, and full of integrity…

What these charlatans are actually selling though, is snake oil and elixirs.

Within the walls of type of agent, everyone is in on the act from the receptionist to the CEO.

It's all part of their plan to keep the properties coming in.

At an interview for a very well-known brand, the COO of this business said to me, **"Why do you care so much what a seller gets…"**

Here's how they work.

The 'Unethicals' will arrange as many viewings as they can. It doesn't matter whether a buyer asked to see your home or not. The buyer was being taken there anyway to make it look like the agent is working hard for you.

Next step...

TELL THE SELLER THE MARKET ISNT QUITE LIKE WHAT THEY THOUGHT IT WAS...

Say the market isn't quite like they thought it was → no offers, they'll try to convince you, the only option is to reduce your initial asking price pressurising you to reduce, until finally you accept a below market value offer...

The 'unethicals' biz model is only concerned about selling long contracts to fulfil their financial dreams and using your property to hit their KPI's not matter what they need to say to achieve it.

These people are wolves in sheep's clothing and would steal the eyes out of your head if you weren't looking.

The problem for you is that the morning your property appears online you go to market, you don't get a second chance to make a first impression.

These agents know this.

But…

They also know that if they tell you the truth of what your property is really worth, the race to winning your instruction (signature on a contract) will stand a very good chance of failing.

So convince themselves…

Your life…

Your journey…

Your next chapter, isn't of any concern to them.

They've learnt not to care.

In other words…

Showing you how to truly maximise the real value of your home is the last thing on their agenda.

Instead, they deliberately chose tactics and strategies that cost homeowners thousands of pounds in lost revenue on the real value of their home's.

What I'm going to say may sting you a little.

The truth is.

Sellers more often than not, go with the agent that gave the highest marketing figure and disregard the agent who said the least, assuming the agent who said the least doesn't know their market.

...or accused of trying to undersell to one of his developer mates or sell cheap to make a quick buck...

So how do you tell the difference between the professionals, Dishonourables and Unethicals?

In this book, I'm gonna reveal to you exactly how...

After that...

...the rest is in your hands.

THE RULES [TRUTHS] OF THE GAME

TRUTH #1 - AN ESTATE AGENT IS A RENTED ASSET AND LIKE ANY PIECE OF RENTED EQUIPMENT, IF IT'S NOT PERFORMING MAKE SURE IT CAN BE HANDED BACK WITHOUT PENALTY

TRUTH #2 – IT'S NOT THE PROMISE OF A PRICE THAT ACHIEVES THE HIGHEST NET PROFIT. IT'S THE PROCESS

TRUTH #3 - PROPERTY IS NOT IN ISOLATION. IT'S IN COMPETITION

TRUTH #4 – A PROPERTY THAT IS WORTH WHAT SOMEONE IS WILLING TO PAY FOR IT, IS WORTH MORE TO COMPETING BUYERS

TRUTH #5 - RIGHT SYSTEM + RIGHT SALESPEOPLE = OUTSTANDING SUCCESS

TRUTH #6 - BUYERS ARE MORE MOTIVATED BY WHAT THEY WILL NOT BE ABLE TO GET IF THEY DONT BUY NOW

TRUTH #7 - HIRE RIGHT, BECAUSE THE PENALTIES FOR HIRING WRONG COSTS THOUSANDS

TRUTH #8 - ALL PROPERTIES ARE DIFFERENT. DON'T TREAT THEM THE SAME. TREAT THEM APPROPRIATELY

TRUTH #10 - AGENTS ARE NOT THE EMPLOYER. SELLERS ARE.

TRUTH #11 – YOU DON'T GET A SECOND CHANCE TO MAKE A FIRST IMPRESSION.

"QUICK STORY..."

Despite the best efforts of the selling solicitor trying to ruin the sale, the seller and I ended up becoming good friends.

So much so, she recommended me to a friend who was about to sell.

Just one issue.

The flat was 6.7 miles up the road in Colindale. What did I know about Colindale?

I was selling property in Ladbroke Grove.

I didn't know anything about the schools in Colindale. The transport links in Colindale. The shops in Colindale. I had nothing to go on. I didn't even know where the flat was.

I couldn't help.

But Mark (the seller), was having none of my insecurities and wouldn't accept no for an answer.

A bit of background about Mark's flat.

Firstly, the flat had a short lease which was valued at £28,000 to extend.

Not only that. At £100 per square foot, the refurb was going to cost around £40,000.

My other problem.

I wouldn't be able to get the time off work to sell it. So I needed to find an agency in Colindale that could.

But would my method of selling property work in a different location? I didn't know as I had never done something like this before...

So I went about discovering the wheat from the chaff and found 8 agents operating in Colindale.

Admittedly, I was panicking. What if I didn't find an agent I could rely on? What if I failed?

I needed to understand who they were and what they stood for? I wanted to know what motivated them?

I didn't care at this stage if the agents in Colindale were horrible dirty lying cheats, or whether they were Nobelist of knights.

The only thing I was interested in, wasn't just how honest they were or how they came to their assumption(s). I also wanted to know their plan.

Some of the responses I got from agents went from astonishing at one end of the bullsh*t scale to perplexing at the other end.

One had a great start introducing himself and company. But got agitated when I asked questions!

How on earth would he cope when things get tough during the sale?

Others were selling me fluff talking up the market, and if the market was as good as they were saying, great. They just had to prove it. If the market was bad, they had to show me why it was bad. If there were a lack of buyers, I wanted them to say so.

Of the 8 agents I spoke to. 3 were invited over to value the flat.

The first agent bored the hell out of me. It wasn't that he wasn't a good guy. I just questioned whether he actually wanted to be there... No drive. No determination.

He worried me...

That said, I was impressed with the second agent until he said, "I'd tell 'em (buyers) what I need to, to get a deal through...!"

The last agent, Ronald (Andrews Online in Kingsbury) was a complete professional.

Brutally honest...

His pitch was all about his agency's method of how to maximise the value of their client's property. I loved it.

He got the instruction…

After two weeks of marketing, Ronald arranged 17 viewings and achieved 5 offers.

Eventually, he agreed the sale at £248,000 from a marketing price of £225,000...!

To put how good this was into perspective…

The best flat on the street that had all the bells and whistles. Decent interior. Long lease etc sold for £265,000.

Mark's flat which needed a £28,000 lease extension including £40,000 worth of refurbishment work, should have sold for £200,000…

Why am I telling you this story…?

If homeowners looked at agents like they were candidates interviewing for a job, homeowners would discover the professionals who deliver results amongst the charlatans that sell sole agency contracts.

In other words, I'm gonna give you the questions that reveal the agents that are highly skilled with the track record to back it up in addition to the steps that creates the perfect storm in any market..

In other words …

I'm showing you how to spot the difference between the good (pro's), the bad (Dishonourables) and the ugly (The Unethicals…)

The fact that you're reading this right now, I'm assuming you're the type of person that wants to be represented by an agent who delivers results...

Implement what I will show you here in this book, you'll get the results you deserve.

"MY PROMISE TO YOU..."

My last boss said to me, "Surely if a house is worth £500,000. You'd say £550,000 to get the client?"

"NO! NO! and F**KING NO AGAIN WILL I SAY SOMETHING JUST TO WIN AN INSTRUCTION BASED ON BULLSHIT!!!"

Where was my tribe? Why can't I keep my feelings in check? Why does bullsh*t affect me so much? Why can't I just fall in line?

When I presented to him how to achieve maximum money for homeowners, all I got was a blank stare…

The best my colleagues could offer, *"Homeowners out here won't accept the London way of doing business!"*

You couldn't make this sh*t up.

Not too long after, I was instructed on a three-bedroom detached located in a floodplain...

That said, my method (Highest Net Profit Formula) generated 41 enquiries within days of going live on the market.

From those enquiries, we block booked 17 viewings with buyers that were likely to offer.

Up to that point, my colleagues had never seen buyer urgency like this!

My client had bought this house for £530,000 eight months earlier and at the time of the sale, we were in a falling market...

When we agreed the sale 2 weeks later, not only did I pay for myself (agency fees), but the extra money also paid for her solicitor fees, removal costs etc...

"F**k You!" I thought to myself...

In the end, I sold my clients property for £30,000 than she paid for it.

But, I was quickly losing faith in this industry.

I hated it for what it stood for.

I hated the people in it.

I hated the lack of consequences agents didn't face if they failed to deliver on their promises.

I hated the lack of truth.

But worse than anything, I hated myself because I had neither the money nor the resources to continue the fight against unethical and Dishonourable estate agents.

I had lost all hope of making a meaningful impact in this industry.

That is…

Until now…

My promise to you…

If you ask the questions inside this book to every single agent you invite to value your home, not only will you maximise the value of your home…

You will put yourself in complete and total control of the sale of your property at a price point you deserve.

The rest is up to you.

"HOW TO USE THIS BOOK..."

In the following chapters, you will not only discover the '21 Secret Insider Questions' the Unethicals and Dishonourable agents don't want you to know.

I'm giving you the other 8 steps that makes up the whole 9 yards.

The '21 Secret Insider Questions' shows whether an agent has a method that sells every time no matter the market.

These questions will also reveal whether the agents you interview work to project deadlines/project milestones/goals?

You need to know which part of the journey you're on.

This book will help you reveal the agent's company mission, vision and philosophy OR even whether they have one?

This book is your cheat code to discovering agents who deliver you the highest level of service they possibly could.

In your hands right now is the power to truly discover the very best agents that know exactly how to maximise the value of your home…

To your success…

STEP 1 - "6 MONTHS, 1 MILE..."

So, before you go to market, the cornerstone of the perfect sale is to think like a surveyor. Why? Because most, if not all the buyers that will come to view your home will require a mortgage.

And although it's your buyer that pays for the survey, surveyors work for banks and won't leave any stone unturned... especially when it comes to the value.

Which gives you a problem...

Unlike buyers, seller's don't go and view other similar properties local to theirs before they put their property on the market which means they don't hear what homes similar to theirs are really selling for...

Said differently, most agents operate in one of two markets.

1. Stars in your eyes market.
2. The other is what property similar to yours actually sold for market

(Buyers and surveyors operate in market number 2)

But most agents operate in stars in your eye's market.

So before you call agents round to your home, your mission is to get a handle on exactly how much property similar to yours have sold for in the last 6 months within a mile radius of your property.

In other words, think like a surveyor thinks...

Because if the price on the market is too high, buyers will look at you with distain believing you to be greedy and won't want to work with you leaving your property stagnant on the market...

STEP 2 - "CHECK AGENT STATS..."

A fantastic place to start when looking for the best local agent is searching for sold prices of similar property's to yours using Rightmove or zoopla including other property portals like homesearch.co.uk and home.co.uk in addition to the Land Registry

Once you've been to the links above, go on GetAgent's website and type in your postcode.

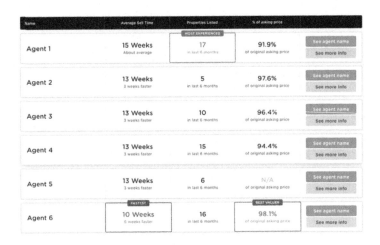

Name	Average Sell Time	Properties Listed	% of asking price	
Agent 1	15 Weeks About average	MOST EXPERIENCED 17 in last 6 months	91.9% of original asking price	See agent name See more info
Agent 2	13 Weeks 3 weeks faster	5 in last 6 months	97.6% of original asking price	See agent name See more info
Agent 3	13 Weeks 3 weeks faster	10 in last 6 months	96.4% of original asking price	See agent name See more info
Agent 4	13 Weeks 3 weeks faster	15 in last 6 months	94.4% of original asking price	See agent name See more info
Agent 5	13 Weeks 3 weeks faster	6 in last 6 months	N/A of original asking price	See agent name See more info
Agent 6	FASTEST 10 Weeks 6 weeks faster	16 in last 6 months	BEST VALUER 98.1% of original asking price	See agent name See more info

To see the agents details, you'll need to add your email address.

As you can see from the above, the agent that is the most convincing is Agent 1. Their valuation accuracy rate is very poor at just 91% compared to agent 6 who delivers most value at 98.1%

Admittedly, not every agent is on GETAGENT, so you'll have to check out reviews of other local Estate Agencies by simply Googling 'Estate Agents Near Me.'

Add Step 1 to this step and you'll start to build a solid picture of who the 'INTERESTED IN' are vs the 'EXPERT IN' who actually deliver results.

Agent 6 also has the best average sell time of all the agents above at 10 weeks. And although the best of the bunch, their still not great. Property should be under offer within 30 days of coming to market...

STEP 3 - "ASK THE RIGHT QUESTIONS..."

So most, if not all sellers are not privy to how much properties are really selling for other than seeing what other similar property's to theirs are being marketed for.

So not their fault because we trust agents to tell us the truth when it comes to valuing our homes.

[Go to www.zerobsestateagency.com/21questions to download your free 21 questions score sheet]

But most Agent's won't tell the truth because they fear losing instructions.

So when it comes to saying a figure, they use phrases like, *"I suggest putting your property on the market for X price to fully test the market."*

"...to fully test the market." is agent code for we've just overvalued your property to win your instruction.

Unfortunately, it's a tactic used to get you to sign a long contract you can't get out of.

Below are the 21 questions with answers.

But, if I were limited to just 4 questions to make sure I'm weeding out the unethical agents to minimise my risk, I'll ask the agents these 4 questions.

1. How much should I market my property for?
2. How much, in your opinion, is my property worth?
3. What price point will get your 10 very best buyers round here right now?
4. If you fail to deliver on your price promise, will you sell my property for free?

Answer's 2 and 3 shouldn't be different from the first answer.

If it is, you're being bullsh*tted to.

The agents you've invited should provide you with the comparable evidence of what's sold similar to yours within the last 6 months and within a 1-mile radius.

You're trying the discover not only who will represent the sale of your home the best, but also has a resume and the proof that they can effectively project manage the sale of your home...

Seriously, treat selling your home like a project. Employing the agent is the recruitment phase.

SECRET INSIDER QUESTION #1

"If you win my instruction, how much do you suggest we market my property for...?"

Seriously, get the price wrong and you can kiss goodbye what you want to happen in your next property chapter of your life...

Tom Panos, one of Australia's most well-respected agents said recently, *"If you go too high on the price, you'll have an overpriced turkey and the owner would say, "you told me that you would get me that price!"*

He went on, *"But if you say exactly what it's worth, most of the time, it's lower than what the owner wants..."*

Panos explains there are three figures when selling: The *Emotional, The Probable and The Mathematical.*

"The *Emotional* price is where someone falls in love with your home and would do anything to get it. Or for example, the neighbour that has just split with her partner. She has a 5-year-old (and with parents that'll help financially), they'll pay more for your home than a general buyer.

But that relies on a relationship breaking down.

Not a good strategy right.

"Then there's the *Probable* figure. This is the figure that is based on comparable evidence compared against what other similar properties that have sold for. This is where surveyors working on behalf of banks operate.

They're only be interested in sold prices within the last 6 months for properties similar to yours within a 1 mile radius.

If there's no proof, the surveyor won't sign it off and the bank won't be lending your buyer the money to buy your home.

"And the third figure is the Mathematical figure…" Panos states, *"Buyers at this level are where bargain hunters operate".*

In other words, marketing your property at the emotional figure, you'll only end up 9.9 times out of 10 attract bargain basement offers.

Why?

Because buyers won't buy what other buyers don't want…

SECRET INSIDER QUESTION #2

"What Percentage of Asking Price Do You Achieve on Average For Your Seller's...?"

The closer to 100% of their original suggested asking price an Agent is, the more integrity they have.

This is the easiest question to answer of all the 21 questions if the agents you're talking to really do put their clients first...

An agent that on average achieves 95% and below, you're speaking with a snake oils salesman. 96% is the UK average (aka shockingly bad). 97% is above the national average but nowhere close to being okay. 98% valuation accuracy is heading in the right direction and 99% equates to massive levels of integrity and professionalism.

My average is 99.47%

So when an agent tells you how well their agency is performing and how they've sold more local property than any other agent in the local area...

All that's great.

But if their valuation accuracy rate is 96% are they the type of agent that would fight for every penny your property deserves or are they only interested in selling you a lengthy contract?

The point I'm making...

No matter how nice an agent's word's sound, their numbers speak for themselves.

The closer to 100% valuation accuracy rate the better they perform and the better your selling journey will be.

On the other hand, the further away from 100% equates to a lack of skill and knowledge...

But most of all, a massive lack of integrity...

SECRET INSIDER QUESTION #3

"How many days are your properties on the market before they go under offer...?"

No word of a lie, you should be under offer within 30 days of coming to market.

An agent's sole aim should be deliberately positioning your property to attract as many ready, willing and able buyers as possible to compete for your home.

The UK average of days on market is 168 days!

Like WTF!!

1 day beyond 30 days, there better be a good reason.

But 168 days and beyond, you're speaking with an agent that doesn't know what they're doing or the more likely version, they're knowingly locking you into a 60 to 200 day sole agency contract you can't get out of.

But why is 30 days the benchmark?

Because to the buying public, a property sitting on the market for longer than 30 looks like there could be something wrong with it.

Remember, you don't get a second chance to make a first impression when your home goes to market.

Property that does go under offer within 30 days of coming to market, isn't priced cheap. It's priced right and more importantly, puts you in control of the selling journey, not agents that prey on the vulnerable...

SECRET INSIDER QUESTION #4

"What has your VIEWING to OFFER ratio been in the last 12 months...?"

When I first started in this industry, I showed buyers what they asked to go and see.

Sounds normal right.

You want to go and see a property, I'll show you.

Thing is...

Showing buyers what they asked to go and see got me more complaints than offers...

Literally, buyers complained to my manager that I was showing them the wrong properties.

"But how could I be!?" I would ask.

THEY ASKED TO SEE WHAT I SHOWED THEM!

The truth is, I didn't know what I was doing...

Said differently, if you were a client of mine, you would have been spending ages making your home look pristine for buyers that had little to no intention of purchasing your home.

I literally didn't qualify buyers good enough and was letting my sellers down.

Fact is, every buyer an agent brings to view your home should be coming with a view to making you an offer…

Today, I point blank refuse to show a buyer a property if they're not right for it.

But what if an agency is bringing Tom, Dick and Harry deliberately?

How would you really know in advance that this is their business model designed to get you to reduce later…

The beauty of question #4, is that you now know, every buyer an agent brings to your home should be coming with a view to making you an offer.

If they don't offer, why?

And if the agency doesn't know what their viewing to offer ratio is…

That's because of 2 things…

1. The office negotiators don't know how to properly qualify buyers and are simply door openers…
2. It's part of the show, and all the agents inside the office are in on the act looking acting like they don't know why no one's offering…

Either way…

...Run!

SECRET INSIDER QUESTION #5

"How many properties have you been instructed to sell and how many of these have you completed on in the last 12 months...?"

According to Rightmove, a whooping 60% of sellers end up selling their home through the second agent!

Florent Lambert, Director of Estate Agency Home Domus 360 in Essex wrote is area, *"Across Essex I find that the average sale ratio over 12 months is about 40% but only about 15% of agents achieve a sale ratio over 50% and only about 3% over 65%*

Of purple bricks he said, "…despite taking the money early and therefore keeping their customers for longer, Purplebricks only achieve just over the average around 42-44% sale ratio over a 12 months period.

"The large corporate chains of estate agents do deliver a poor sale ratio, Bairstow Eves and Abbotts among the worst ones."

But in my experience, a seller deciding not to sell after going to market is rare.

Yes, things change.

Yes people decide not to sell for whatever reason.

But the reason so many property sales full through is because they were won based on lies and deceit, not integrity and professionalism.

Said differently...

Property doesn't fail to sell because sellers and buyers intentions change.

More often than not, it's because the agents set the sales price, positioning and promotion completely wrong.

Remember, although agents wield great power in a property sale, they are still a very small cog in the property market.

And an agent that can't be exact with you about how many instructions they've won versus how many they've sold, why don't they know their numbers?

My rolling average is almost 1 in 1.

SECRET INSIDER QUESTION #6

"How many properties have you sold at the asking price or above in the last 12 months...?"

Below are my marketing prices in the left green column vs. what I achieved in the right green column with the percentage achieved in the right-hand column.

Property	Marketing Price	Achieved	%
47 Eynham Road	£ 485,000	£485,000.00	100.00
93 West Row	£ 349,950	£334,000.00	95.44
4 Malvern Close	£ 850,000	£850,000.00	100.00
20 Chesterton Road	£ 610,000	£615,000.00	100.82
12 Croft House	£ 300,000	295000.00	98.33
24 Lothrop Road	£ 775,000	£735,000.00	94.84
15a Eynham Road	£ 725,000	£725,000	100.00
61 Lancaster Road	£ 440,000	£420,000.00	95.45
12c St Marks Place	£ 280,000	£280,000.00	100.00
92 Cambridge Gardens	£ 550,000	£500,000.00	90.91
4 Nascot Street	£ 550,000	£525,000.00	95.45
84 Cambridge Gardens	£ 450,000	£450,000.00	100.00
25 Kilravock Street	£ 750,000	£715,000.00	95.33
166 Ladbroke Grove	£ 550,000	£550,000.00	100.00
59 Lowerwood Court	£ 325,000	£340,000.00	104.62
231 Ladbroke Grove	£ 275,000	£275,000.00	100.00

Pav Terrace	£ 499,999	£491,000.00	98.20
58 Noko	£ 460,000	£450,000.00	97.83
77 Noko	£ 410,000	£390,000.00	95.12
46 Noko	£ 420,000	£400,000.00	95.24
76 Noko	£ 420,000	£400,000.00	95.24
37 Noko	£ 395,000	£420,000.00	106.33
228 LG	£ 550,000	£540,000.00	98.18
33 Bartholomew House	£ 425,500	£422,500.00	99.29
15 James House	£ 375,000	£375,000.00	100.00
73 Bramley Road	£ 225,000	£251,750.00	111.89
1 James House	£ 385,000	£395,000.00	102.60
98h Cambridge Gardens	£ 450,000	£450,000.00	100.00
27 St Andrews	£ 730,000	£730,000.00	100.00
144 Kilburn Lane	£ 775,000	£750,000.00	96.77
Flat 3 40 Bassett Road	£ 690,000	£690,000.00	100.00
125 Ladbroke Grove	£ 650,000	£705,000.00	108.46
25 Bartholomew	£ 385,000	£410,000.00	106.49
59 Tavistock Cres	£ 425,000	£ 400,000	94.12
11 Noko	£ 460,000	£ 475,000	103.26
13 Noko	£ 460,000	£ 475,000	103.26
35 Noko	£ 500,000	£ 500,000	100.00
48 St Lawrence	£ 600,000	£ 617,000	102.83
345 347 Ladbroke Grove	£ 350,000	£353,000.00	100.86
F3 61 Lancaster Road	£450,000	£450,000.00	100.00
104 Lancaster Road	£ 685,000	£670,000.00	97.81

| 16 Bartholomew House | £ 500,000 | £500,000.00 | 100.00 |
| 4 Garnet Court, Marlow | £ 535,000 | £560,000.00 | 104.67 |

So why is question #6 important?

Because what sort of sale would you like when selling?

One where you're in control of the entire selling process or one where days and weeks turn into months of sitting stagnant on the market?

The question to have in the back of your mind before you employ n agent to represent you... *"Is this agency attempting to deliberately position my property to attract the very best buyers to compete for my signature or are they just saying things that sound nice to win my instruction?"*

Because as you'll have just seen.

I don't always get it right.

The difference is, I will sell your home for free should I fail to deliver on my price promise.

SECRET INSIDER QUESTION #7

"Can you explain in detail what other properties similar to mine have sold for and when...?"

'What Agent's Want You To Believe When Selling Your Home...'

Start Line   Finish Line

In the illustration above, unethical and the dishonourable agents give the impression that the house selling journey is the easiest thing in the world.

Put the house on at the "Emotional Figure". Bob's your uncle. Fanny's ya Aunt. Bish Bash Bosh, job's a good'un. Sell for massive money and you don't even have to be good at it.

It's easy...

But… is this really the case?

Surveyors, mortgage companies and banks scrutinise every last piece of data to make sure they're lending on a property they can get their money back should the buyer default on their mortgage.

They need to be sure of the value the property is being sold.

Which means surveyors will not sign off on a property's value if they can't find evidence of an agent's claims…

It's more than their job's worth.

If an agent can't prove what other properties similar to yours have sold for, your potential buyer and their lender will down-value your property.

The reality for most sellers is having to continually climb mountains with no end in sight. The below illustration is the reality for most sellers when selling...

'The Reality...'

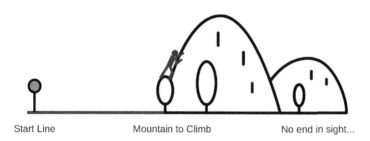

Start Line   Mountain to Climb   No end in sight...

Put another way, if a lender doesn't have comparable evidence confirming your property is worth what the buyer has agreed to pay, they may still offer a mortgage, but not at the level a buyer needs it to be in order to proceed which rarely ends well for sellers.

So you want proof that what the agent is telling you is tangible.

Think like a surveyor thinks.

The current rule of thumb that surveyors work with…

Completed properties (similar to yours) sold within the last 6 months and within a mile radius of your property.

In the meantime, check out these property websites if you haven't already seen them. Loads of valuable information.

www.getagent.co.uk

www.home.co.uk

www.homesearch.co.uk

SECRET INSIDER QUESTION #8

"How will local, national and international economies affect the sale of my property...?"

The simple answer is…

==>A lot.

Many economies and sectors including political landscape will affect the sale of your home, not just your local area.

At an international level, it could be oil & gas, money markets, international elections, politics, natural disasters, war...

Nationally, you might have the High Speed 2 rail link tunnelling directly under your home…

Maybe planning permission has just been granted for 1000 new properties to be built on your doorstep over the next 7 to 10 years.

British Steel going into administration, or the state of car manufacturing will also affect the sale of your home.

Does the agent you're talking to know the answers to these questions?

Fact is…

All the above has the potential to negatively affect the sale of your home.

These are the exact same questions your potential buyers will be asking including their solicitor, the bank of mum and dad, terry down the pub, Amelie in the office...

Everyone will have an opinion.

If you've done your homework and the agent tries to bullsh*t you, how will they be representing you?

Make sure you take the time to study unrelated markets including what's happening at home and abroad.

Any agent that doesn't share this information with you is either negligent or worse, they don't know.

Remember...

Information is power.

And having this information will empower you irrespective of negative or potential scary information that comes to light before or during your house sale.

SECRET INSIDER QUESTION #9

"Mr Agent, what questions do you ask buyers to be absolutely confident they will make me an offer before they come to my home...?"

As I mentioned above, when I first started in the industry, I got more complaints than offers.

I literally got everything wrong, and my colleagues hovered over me like vultures...

I cringe now, but back then I'd ask buyers questions like what they did for a living or how much deposit they had...

My questioning had nothing to do with their dreams or aspirations.

I found out the hard way that knowing how much deposit a buyer has, has never and never will have an impact on selling a client's home.

Asking 'details' questions like 'do they have a deposit?' or whether they have a solicitor' are questions agents should want the answer to, but agents make buyers feel like they're being interrogated.

I was regularly pissing people off by asking stupid questions that nothing to do with a buyer's dreams...

Which lead to another nasty side effect.

I was unable to give sellers' feedback; other than the potential buyer didn't like the curtains or the colours of the wall.

Imagine I brought a potential buyer to your home and all I could tell you was that the buyers are from Basildon. They work and have a deposit of 20% and a mortgage in principle.

Compared to...

"One of the couples coming to view your home (Sally and David) have just missed out on a property exactly like yours. However, from the pictures and floorplan, your home looks like it could work better for them and their two children.

Not just that, your kitchen is pretty much the perfect size which means they don't have to extend.

Their kids are young, so being on a no-through road works perfectly.

They're currently in rented accommodation on a month's notice so should your property work for them, they'll be happy to work with you re-timings as they know you haven't found your new home yet."

In real life, I'd get a lot more information about what they want than above.

But, the more information about a person's reasons 'why' they want to view your home, the more likely they will make you an offer.

For example, what was the purpose of the buyer's call? Why did they want to come and see your home?

Let me be clear.

I wouldn't accept a buyer being shown my home if all the information the agent could get from them was that they had a job and were from Basildon.

Neither should you.

When agents are qualifying buyers, they should be building a buyer profile based on...

1) **Why this buyer?**

2) **Why your home?**

Not every buyer will offer. But the more the agent knows, the more likely a buyer will offer.

The point I'm making...

If an agent starts 'erming' and 'arghing' when you ask this question, it means they don't have a predictable and profitable process of qualifying buyers...

'Erming' and 'arghing' must be shown the door.

SECRET INSIDER QUESTION #10

"Who will be responsible for updating me on viewing feedback and deal progression once I'm under offer...?

Most of the time, the person responsible for updating the seller is the negotiator whose buyer (also known as an *Applicant*), won the right to buy a seller's home.

But...

What if this is the negotiator's first job out of school?

What if the agency they're working for doesn't educate their employees on the process of buying and selling houses?

What if their training consists of, "There's a desk. There's a phone. Get on the calls..."

If this is the case, they're 'learning on your dime...'

But when it comes to selling someone's property, 'learning on a sellers dime or learning on the job' is like giving a 17-year-old babysitter permission to take your £10 million vintage Ferrari out for a ride without a licence...

Literally.

That's who you could end up trusting to be in control of your most prized asset...

The person responsible for giving you feedback doesn't have to be the director or owner of the business, or even a manager.

But it must be someone who has a provable track record of results of keeping entire chains together and getting deals across the finish line.

There will be so many people involved in getting the sale of your property through to completion, from other agents to solicitors, to mortgage brokers, and each with varying skill levels.

Not only does the office neg (negotiator) representing you have to project manage all of the above personalities, they've also gotto manage an entire chain of properties.

But maybe the negotiator who's just started out will be struggling to hold their own hand, let alone being able to guide you or others in the chain of a thousand links.

Put another way, the person dealing with your sale must play many roles.

Mother. Father. Counsellor. Teacher. Estate Agent. Hostage Negotiator. Sage…

Said differently...

If they don't have skill and experience, they'll get eaten alive.

Not just by the thousand links in the chain, but by their colleagues. By their boss. By other sellers. Buyers. Solicitors. By the process and other peoples systems which will lead to overwhelm first. Then procrastination. Then they'll stop answering your calls.

The list goes on.

So the answer to this question is: make sure you're 100% certain the person looking after you either has bags of provable skill experience of successfully selling houses through previous client testimonials.

PS. at the very minimum, they should be updating you once per week whether you're property is under offer or not and many more times in-between.

SECRET INSIDER QUESTION #11

"What are your sole agency fees…?"

So there are three types of agency fees.

1. Pull Your Pants Down
2. The Absolute Minimum.
3. An Excellent Alternative

Pull Your Pants Down

Pulling your pants down fee is agent that doesn't know how to protect the value of what they offer so they pull their pants down.

"What was that. The agent said they'll sell your home for 1%, I'll sell it for 0.75%…"

If they're easily persuaded to drop their fee to sell your home, my question is, what will they say when to a prospective buyer who tries to low ball you?

Will they? Can they? Are they skilled enough to protect the price of your property's price?

Or will they try to convince you to accept the low ball offer instead?

You can't be the best agent in the area and charge the lowest fee…

The Absolute Minimum Fee.

So my absolute fee is 1.5% and here's why…

A giant ship's engine failed.

The ship's owners tried one expert after another, but none of them could figure but how to fix the engine.

Then they brought in an old man who had been fixing ships since he was a young. He carried a large bag of tools with him, and when he arrived, he immediately went to work. He inspected the engine very carefully, top to bottom.

Two of the ship's owners were there, watching this man, hoping he would know what to do.

After looking things over, the old man reached into his bag and pulled out a small hammer and gently tapped something.

Instantly, the engine lurched into life. He carefully put his hammer away. The engine was fixed!

A week later, the owners received a bill from the old man for ten thousand dollars.

"What?!" the owners exclaimed. "He hardly did anything!"

So they wrote the old man a note saying, "Please send us an itemized bill."

The man sent a bill that read:

Tapping with a hammer......£ 2.00

Knowing where to tap.........£ 9,998.00

Said differently

Effort is important but knowing where to make an effort makes all the difference!

But can I prove the above?

- Percentage of asking price I achieve compared to my competition?
- Do I have a marketing methodology that delivers results versus what my competition achieves?
- Do I have a superior viewing to offer ratio than my competition?
- Can I prove my instructed to sales completion ratio?
- What's my valuation accuracy rate? Can I prove it's superior to other local agents?
- Do I insist on investing in professional photography or will try to convince you that taking pictures with my kodak is acceptable?
- Have I taken you through a detailed list of all the similar properties on the market within 5 miles of your home and what they sold for and when?
- Have I been able to detail the exact pounds per square other property is selling for similar to yours within a five-mile radius?
- Have I shared with you how many competing offers my methodology achieves?

An Excellent Alternative

An excellent alternative is a sliding scale.

In other words, the better the agents does for you, the more they earn...

Equally...

The worse they do, the less they get paid.

For example...

- **1.5% fee at a provable marketing figure of £500,000**

- **£25,000 above the provable value, the agent gets paid 1.75%**

- **But if the agent achieves £475,000 their fee dramatically reduces to 0.5%**

The point I'm making...

Agent's that claim to be the best local agent but charge the lowest fee aren't the best agents.

Said differently, if they can't protect their own fee, will they have the determination and courage to protect you?

Here's the truth, the higher an agent's valuation is and the closer their fee is to zero, the less likely it is they have a blueprint, methodology or formula for maximising a seller's profits.

An agent whose valuation accuracy rate is at or very slightly below 100% is a 2% percent agent.

SECRET INSIDER QUESTION #12

"Do you insist all your clients have their property professionally photographed...?"

You could have the worst looking home or the most stunning looking home. Either way, your property needs to be seen in its best light which is where professional photography comes in.

Interestingly, pro photography isn't for you. Pro photography is for your potential buyers...

It's for their friends. Their Colleagues. Their Solicitor. Their Lender. The lender's surveyor, the bank of Mum and Dad.

You need to make all of the above love your home when you come to sell.

Everyone else connected to a buyer through work or friendship needs to be just as excited and enthusiastic as your buyer.

Professional photography in estate agency is a minimum 50% of the battle in achieving a successful sale.

It means as much as that.

Sounds mental, but pro photography is a must.

Don't take any sh*t from an agent that says otherwise.

Get them to use professional Pro photography even if that means you have for pro photography yourself.

SECRET INSIDER QUESTION #13

"What strategy does your agency employ to maximise the value of the properties on your books...?"

Straight off the bat, if an agent doesn't tell you their strategy that maximises the value of their client's property, be afraid. Be very afraid.

Because without a strategy your property won't be perceived as one of a kind. It'll look like everything else on the market.

When valuing and discussing how to maximise the value of a client's home, being open with a seller about what I really think, especially if it's going to be seen as a negative, is a hard thing to do.

Most agents don't want to offend, so they choose popularity over having the guts to say what's right...

And the problem with being popular, it costs homeowners thousands of pounds.

When I'm valuing a seller's home, I ask them, **"How are you going to get every potential buyer to stop what they're doing and get them to come to your home instead?"**

In other words...

If you can accept your property is 100% in competition with other similar properties on the market within a 5 mile radius, you will achieve maximum results every time....

Ask the agent what their strategy is?

Do they have a strategy that they can demonstrate that consistently achieves superior results against their competitors?

SECRET INSIDER QUESTION #14

"In your opinion, what is the value of my property? And can you provide comparable evidence of actual and recently sold properties supporting your valuation...?"

With this question, you're beginning to reveal the **skilled agent versus the unskilled agent.**

The **ethical agent versus the unethical agent.**

The **integrity-driven agent versus those with a lack of integrity.**

If the agent you're speaking to does not (or cannot) provide evidence to confirm what he's saying, he's bullsh*tting you in an attempt to use your home to keep his office doors open as opposed to using his agency to open doors for you.

Equally, if he or she is able to show you evidence backing up their valuation with a good number of property details, then perfect! They're not bullsh*tting you.

Remember. 6 months. 1 mile radius.

But...

Do not be fooled by an *"on the market"* price. You need to see actual sold prices within the last 6 months within a 1-mile radius.

Remember, only properties sold within the last 6 months and within a mile of your property will be considered proof by Surveyors.

On a TikTok Live, I was asked what is the single killer question to ask estate agents at a valuation?

There are actually 4 (remember what I mentioned above).

1. **"How much is my property worth...?"**
2. **"How much do you suggest I market my property for...?"**
3. **"What price will get the 10 very best buyers round to my home right now...?"**
4. **"If you won my instruction, will you sell my property for free should you fail to deliver on your price promise...?"**

The price difference between question 1 and 3 shouldn't be different and the agent that says they'll absolutely sell your house for free (#4) is the agent who's being must truthful and the one that you can trust.

SECRET INSIDER QUESTION #15

"Can you tell me exactly how many buyers you have actively looking for a property like mine at the price point you've suggested...?"

If you were with me, we were 10 minutes away from jumping into the unknown. Tensions. Aggression. The blokes became more and more violent in their attempts to find an inch of space in the packed fuselage of an RAF C-130 Hercules...

I was part of an entire battle group of a thousand paratroopers taking part in a three-week exercise in Scotland.

We were jumping at 130mph from 243 meters above the ground.

Most of the blokes at that time were already battle-hardened from tours in Kosovo and Sierra Leonne.

Yet, these robust battle-hardened soldiers were vomiting into sick bags...

Not only that, but we were also exiting the aircraft with 180lbs of equipment strapped to us.

Looking out the portside door I was the 22nd man, allowing me to see two other Hercules C-130's with their first men in their door's looking back at us.

It was like a scene from a film.

The plane rose to 800ft.

The RED light came to life…

5 seconds later, "GREEN ON…!"

GO! GO! GO!

In rapid succession, paratroopers were exiting the aircraft one after the other…

By this time, I had done 13 jumps in my army career and was a little more worried than normal.

My worry wasn't jumping.

My worry was missing the Drop Zone.

Missing the Drop Zone by just a few seconds in a plane doing 130mph meant landing a lifetime away from where we should have been dropped. Especially having to carry 180Ibs!

Half the blokes had managed to get out the door, then suddenly, the plane lost power.

The blokes that were still on the plane including myself were thrown all over the place.

Yet the Loadmaster at the door was still screaming GO! GO! GO!

Somehow I made it out the door…

ONE THOUSAND. TWO THOUSAND. THREE THOUSAND. CHECK CANOPY...

As soon as my chute opened, I saw the sky below was filled with paratroopers that jumped about 10 to 15 seconds before my wave.

As I looked up, another wave of paratroopers exited their aircrafts.

At that moment there were well over 1000 chutes in the sky.

Just like a brigade jump, buyers also come in waves.

Wave One: Agents should have at least five to seven buyers actively looking for a property like yours at the price point they've told you.

Wave Two: These are buyers the agent doesn't know. They're actively looking but will only raise their hand if they agree with the marketing price.

Wave Three. If you're relying on this wave of buyers, you'll have a serious problem as these buyers may not even turn up at all.

Let me explain.

Before an agent comes to your home, they already know who on their books is likely to make you an offer (That is of course if they've qualified their buyers properly), which may be just one or two buyers which is fine.

So, if they tell you they have seven buyers lined up and only two people come to view your home in the first week and you don't get an offer, the agent has over-valued your property.

Thing is...

Your agent must attract all three waves of buyers to your home at the same time.

So...

"Mr agent, how many buyers do you have actively looking for a property like mine at the price point you've told me?"

If they don't know the exact number that's a big problem.

SECRET INSIDER QUESTION #16

"Is your valuation the figure I'm likely to achieve...?"

Now we're getting to the heart of whether agent has integrity or not, as this question is designed to the give the agent no room for manoeuvre, because they've already giving a figure in **INSIDER QUESTION #14.**

The answer is a simple YES or NO?

If they say "hmmm, well, erm…" you will have just freaked them out and you'll have discovered whether they're really that confident about the first figure they gave you?

Remember all these questions are designed to put you in total control of the sale of your home, not the agent.

The agent that truly has your best interests at heart is the difference between an amateur focusing on making sales (selling you a long and drawn out contract) versus a professional that focuses on achieving you the highest net profit.

If they're full of sh*t, this question will reveal it.

SECRET INSIDER QUESTION #17

"On average, how many competing offers per property do you generate for your clients' properties...?"

Creating a situation where there are competing offers on every property is nowhere near guaranteed, but it's the target all agents should be looking to achieve for their sellers.

Always!

In the previous question they confirmed to you the price you should sell for.

Okay, cool.

Now let them show you the evidence of how many competing offers they generate...

Agents should have a library of stats from the number of viewings they achieve per property, to how many people they called about it. How many buyers offered on each of their properties to the price it sold for compared against the price it was marketed at.

They should use this information to spot trends in their local market.

You'll want to see this information too.

This information is key for two reasons.
1. To understand exactly how much your property is worth and
2. selling for more than your property is worth.

To truly sell for much more than the market value, you need to get buyers to compete.

And to achieve this, properties need to be bang on the money with their marketing price.

The fact is, you don't need competing offers to achieve the market value.

The reason you want competing offers is not just to give you the ability to achieve over the asking price for your home, but also to make sure if your property sale falls out of bed with one buyer you can easily replace with the next buyer…

In other words,

…you can replace the sale without losing a wink of sleep...

SECRET INSIDER QUESTION #18

"How many weeks is your minimum term contract, and does it contain a notice period...?"

77 days after accepting an offer, the agent finally admitted the buyer he introduced couldn't get a mortgage!

Steve, a friend of mine from my Parachute Regiment days, was furious.

He and his wife were spending lots of money on solicitors fees. Mortgage fees and various other surveys in an attempt to buy their dream home.

Yet for almost three months their agent failed to tell them the buyer wasn't in a position to proceed!

Steve had pretty much done what everyone else connected with the sale had asked him to do...

He told me, "My missus wanted an explanation from him (the agent) as to why the buyers were allowed to go 11 weeks without being picked up for no mortgage?"

The agent told her it was not his responsibility! But in fact, it was the buyer's solicitor's responsibility to inform Steve and his wife...

WHAT... THE...!

Point to note if this happens to you.

This is not the job of the solicitor. And even if it was, the agent should be all over it regardless...

So many times, sales have unnecessarily fallen out of bed because agents are not checking whether a buyer is proceedable (a buyer with a mortgage in principle doesn't make them proceedable) leaving sellers to miss out on their dream homes because of lacklustre 'can't be arsed' performance...

Equally, the agent dealing with the sale doesn't know what they're doing.

The point I'm making...

When Steve tried to dis-instruct his agent, they enforced a 28-day notice period.

W...T...F...!

They literally failed to chase or mention that Steve's buyer did not have a mortgage for 11 weeks, yet felt they were entitled to get paid?

To be clear, it's the agent's job to make sure everybody involved knows what's going on at all times from the first to the last link in the chain.

...and I mean everyone.

The point I'm making. Don't sign a contract that lasts more than 30 days.

A 30-day contract is long enough.

10 to 12-week contracts are designed to keep you locked in so you can't go to another agent and equally, it enables an agent to beat you down on their deliberate over estimation later...

Good agents will have no problem with a 30-day contract.

Why?

Because they understand exactly what they're doing.

I can't stress this enough. A correctly priced property will be under offer within a matter of weeks of coming to market.

Said differently...

Don't be the seller that finds themselves in Steve's position that you cannot get out of.

On the contract, write 30 days and cross out the 28 day notice period and get the agent to sign the page to acknowledge what they've agreed.

SECRET INSIDER QUESTION #19

"When a buyer makes me an offer, how will your estate agency present it to me…?"

Imagine for a moment, you've been told, "You know the most amazing couple who viewed your home on Saturday. The couple in the most incredible buying position… Well… they are going to make you an offer!"

You were assured they were so perfect; you accepted their offer and excitedly called your other half to tell them the news.

You employed a highly recommended solicitor.

You paid your lender to carry out a full structural survey on your next home…

A week passes and you're still waiting for news on when your buyers' survey is taking place.

Three weeks have now passed, and your buyer's solicitor still hasn't asked your solicitor a single question. Yet your solicitor is flying - the searches are back, and a written mortgage offer is in the post.

Five weeks have now passed, and you've been told that the buyer has paid for their survey, but it still hasn't been booked in.

Meanwhile, the buyer's solicitor still hasn't been in contact with yours????

Where's your agent?!

Your agent should be showing you proof that anyone offering really are in a position to proceed.

So what do you need to see?

- Firstly, confirmation in writing (letter or email) from the buyer's lender that they have a mortgage in principle. (MIP's mean nothing by the way. Not the buyer's fault. It just shows the buyer has taken the time to speak to a lender.)

- Confirmation in writing from the buyer's solicitor that they have been instructed to act on the buyer's behalf.

- Actual proof that your potential buyer has the required deposit. i.e. cash in the bank. (Not money tied up in a vague investment fund).

- Confirmation in writing from the buyer that they can work to your timeframes to complete the sale.

Why would the Agent show you all of this?

Because your agent works for you and if they are managing the sale properly, (especially if it is part of a chain) their role is to make sure all parties across the entire chain are aware of progress and agree to work to deadlines.

Selling your home is a project and if your agent isn't in control of the project, then you're not.

The agent you employ is responsible for making sure you get the highest possible price, but their first priority should be protecting your future by making sure the person you've agreed to sell to (based on all the evidence presented) will and can work towards purchasing your home in a timeframe your in control of.

Not being shown the details above is as good as your agent taking you hiking across Dartmoor in the dark and without a torch.

They'll get you lost and your sale will die.

SECRET INSIDER QUESTION #20

"How many testimonials can you show me for you personally including members of your office team...?"

Most high street agencies look great on the outside.

Modern. Fresh. Exciting.

Equally, there are some Agencies that from the outside look dishevelled, battered and broken. Paint peeling off the walls and letters missing from the company logo.

Some agents don't even have an office.

Which of the three types of agents above would you use?

Modern, battered or no office?

What if you were thinking of using 'modern and fresh' only to discover 'battered and broke' achieved more superior results...

What if 'battered and broke's average asking price achieved for their homeowners was higher than all of their competition?

What if their clients' properties were snapped up immediately for over the asking price?

What if they expertly put their clients in total control of the selling process?

How would you know?

The point I'm making is this.

Whether the agent looks fresh and exciting or battered and broken, the question to any agent should be, "*can you show me what people are saying about your agency and what they're saying about you and the individual negotiators inside your office?*"

After all, how would you know if the agent's you interview only skillset was the ability to talk a good game?

Agents with nothing to hide would happily show you proof of what people were saying about them.

The point I'm making, if you want to be as sure as you can about the agents you're talking to, it's a completely necessary question to ask.

SECRET INSIDER QUESTION #21

"Should you not deliver on your promises including delivering the figure you said I should expect to achieve, will your agency sell my property for free...?"

Should agents face consequences for poor or misleading advice...? i.e., should they get paid if they fail to deliver you their price promise?

I believe they should sell your home for FREE if they don't deliver on their promises.

Why?

Because agents know exactly what a property is worth. The pros will have the honesty to tell you. 99% won't.

As I've said earlier in the book; the value of a property is not subjective. If it was, banks and mortgage companies would lend on everything, but they do not.

Imagine an agent that looked you in the eyes and promised you what he said was real, but after a month of poor performance his only solution was to push YOU to drop the price?

In my opinion, that would be like paying a bricklayer who told you they were capable of building you a wall but attempted to dig you a driveway instead..

Or a cab driver who failed to deliver you to the destination you asked to go.

Would you pay them?

I wouldn't either.

Yet, based on price reductions we see online, how many agencies get away with non-performance?

All of them...

It's common practice.

But what if an agent guaranteed you that if they failed to deliver on their promises, they would sell your home for free?!

I would love this to be enshrined in legislation. I want it to be an industry wide standard.

Without consequences, unethical agents will continue to sacrifice sellers for their own gain.

And this is why this question is so powerful.

Because with all said and done, this question reveals the truth of what an agent really thinks despite all of the answers they've given you above.

www.zerobsestateagency.com 107

STEP 4 - "PROPERTY INFORMATION..."

When you bought your home, it may have felt the person you were buying from was a bit of a nightmare. Their solicitor may not have been answering your solicitors enquiries laying blame at the seller's feet or at external factors. Equally, the Agent may not have been giving you straight answers because they were winging it. The person you were buying from may have felt it was everybody else's fault as to why things were going so slow...

The reality. It wasn't the sellers fault. It wasn't the buyers fault.

The fault lay at the feet of the process.

This will sound mad...

But the problem with selling property is that very few agents actually know the process of buying and selling property.

Meaning, when sh*t hits the fan, agent's that don't know the buying and selling process won't be able to coach, mould, shape your sale to a successful outcome.

Instead, they'll be driving you straight into a minefield.

So Step 4 is all about preparing your sale well before you go to market.

In other words, don't get caught out by not having the legal side prepared.

Below are the items you're going to have to have organised before you go to market.

- Title Deeds.
- Office Copy Entries
- Property Information Form
- Fixtures, Fittings and Contents Form
- If it's a leasehold, the Leasehold Information Form + Management Pack.
- FENSA Certificate
- Planning Documents
- Building Work Receipts

Organising these documents for your solicitor in advance will not only make selling your home so much smoother. It'll immediately put you in a much better position when it comes to competing for an onward purchase...

Download the entire buying and selling process on a single page so no agent nor any link a potential chain can pull the wool over your eyes by going to www.zerobsestateagency.com/1pageinfographic

STEP 5 - "HOW TO CHOOSE THE RIGHT AGENT..."

Amateur and unethical agents rely on false promises, unrealistic results and distorting of the facts to get your property on their books...

For example, below is a conversation I was having with a seller about an agent who according to the seller was "*a nice chap that has been in the game 20 years...*"

"*What's your route to market..?*" the seller asked the nice chap...

"*His response*" said the seller, "*was obviously the usual suspects of websites, but his route to market isn't the thing that'll sell my house, his database of people already looking for a place like mine is what will sell it... and that the agent isn't interested in cheap offers...*"

Let's break that down...

- The agent said buyers. You ask, "How many?"
- What's going to be different about putting this seller's property on Rightmove and Zoopla compared to all the others agents'

properties that are on Rightmove and Zoopla?

- And what the hell does, "Not interested in cheap offers" really mean? What would that look like in reality?
- And can he quantify his database of buyers? Does he have a pool of buyers in the top draw no other agent knows about?
- Is his data base of buyers worth more than his pricing strategy?
- How big is the data base?

Remember Truth #2 → **"It's not the promise of a price that achieves the highest net profit. It's the process..."**

Name	Average Sell Time	Properties Listed	% of asking price		
Agent 1	16 Weeks 5 weeks slower	5 in last 6 months	96.4% of original asking price	See agent name	See more info
Agent 2	11 Weeks About average	3 in last 6 months	94.9% of original asking price	See agent name	See more info
Agent 3	10 Weeks About average	6 in last 6 months	96.9% of original asking price	See agent name	See more info
Agent 4	FASTEST 8 Weeks 3 weeks faster	MOST EXPERIENCED 10 in last 6 months	96.6% of original asking price	See agent name	See more info
Agent 5	9 Weeks 2 weeks faster	6 in last 6 months	96.2% of original asking price	See agent name	See more info
Agent 6	14 Weeks 5 weeks slower	9 in last 6 months	BEST VALUER 98% of original asking price	See agent name	See more info

If you're wondering who the agent was? It was Agent #4 who valued this property...

But notice Agent 6 who offers the most value at 98.1% compared to the nice chap who achieves on average just 96.6% of his originally suggested asking prices, yet the nice chap is the fastest to convince their sellers to reduce their selling price???

In other words, he's bullsh*tting his way to instructions by giving 'stars in your eyes' valuations, but once instructed, he quickly attempts to convince his seller's to take less than what he said he could achieve..!!

It's so bad, its laughable...

96.6% on £100,000 property is a loss of £3,400...

On a £250,000 property it's a loss of £8,500

And approximately £17,000 loss on a home worth £500,000...

and then you have to pay the agent a fee for the privilege of being bullsh*tted to.

Literally, apart from Agent 6, all of the other agents listed above are playing the same game of 'Stars in Your Eyes Valuations...'

The point I'm making is that seller's could be forgiven when they say agents just slap property's on Rightmove and hope for the best.

I agree...

All but one of the above agents are valuing homes based on what they think their competitors will say, not what the actual value in today's market.

When selling, look out for the agents whose pitch is something completely different to the rest...

Imagine an agent told you this at the valuation stage, *"Before you go to market, it's important to know there will be 3 waves of buyers.*

The first wave is the list of buyers we already have on our books looking for a property like yours...

Then there's a second wave of buyers who we don't yet know...

Then there's the third wave of buyers...

Honestly, if we're relying on the third wave, we're in trouble...

The secret though, is to get all 3 waves into your property at the same time.

So the plan is market your property at or slightly below its provable value.

We'll then hold wave 1 back from viewing your property for 1 to 2 weeks from the day the property goes live online.

This will give us the ability to discover the who the second wave of buyers are...

And as mentioned, we also want to get the third wave to come out to play too at an open house within 10 to 14 days from the day we hit the market online.

And by the way, if I don't achieve the market value for your home, I will sell your property for FREE..."

Accountability vs taking responsibility right...

So to cut a long story short, an agent without a plan is risking your future in favour of securing theirs.

Platforms to get your property on the market are vitally important to get your property seen...

"IF YOU'RE NOT WILLING TO RISK THE USUAL, YOU'LL HAVE TO SETTLE FOR ORDINARY..."

STEP 6 - "BUYER SELLER RELATIONSHIP..."

There is no more important relationship during a sale than that of you and your buyer.

Your relationship must be watertight.

I can almost guarantee at some stage after you've agreed to sell, you will either need your buyer or your buyer will need you, which is why for me, you must be present at the first viewing.

Not for the purpose of negotiating.

Leave that to the agent.

But because every viewing I've ever done where the seller has been home, buyers have asked the seller the exact same questions they asked me before the viewing.

Sellers that were home during viewings initially pissed me off until I quickly realised having the seller home on the first viewing built huge trust.

In other words, buyers and sellers not only built strong connections, but they also trusted me (the agent) more than they'd normally trust an agent, which is vital moving forward.

Only on second viewings I insisted on seller's not being home.

I suggest you do the same too...

Honestly... Apart from open days... I absolutely love the seller being home when bringing a buyer to view their property for the first time.

Literally, if I'm bringing a buyer to your home for the first time, I 100% want you there.

And so should every agent.

"PROFIT IS NOT SOMETHING YOU ADD ON AT THE END. IT IS SOMETHING YOU PLAN FOR IN THE BEGINNING..." AUTHOR UNKNOWN

STEP 7 - "AVOID STARS IN YOUR EYE'S VALUATIONS AT ALL COSTS. HERE'S WHY..."

Circa 2016, I had won an instruction to sell a small mid terraced cottage.

Admittedly, I wasn't the original agent.

I wasn't even the second agent.

I was the last agent the seller had asked for help.

In her eyes, I was a last-ditch attempt to sell her home after her property had spent months stagnating on the market with various agents.

Agents that were all too willing to take her property on, but none it seemed had the guts to tell her the truth…

Her problem was that she was relying on agents who were relying on luck to sell her home.

Worse… she had found her dream home. A property that was rapidly slipping from her hands.

It had been almost a year to the day when the office I was working for valued her property (£60,000 less than the agent she initially went with at £485,000)

The original agent found a buyer £485,000 until the buyer realised, they were paying too much.

The problem now.

The seller was 'Anchored' to the STARS IN YOUR EYES £485,000 and based every subsequent financial decision around £485,000.

And because she was emotionally and mentally anchored to £485,000, she really struggled to give us the instruction, especially when our fee was double that of the other agents, yet we were saying her home was valued far less.

In her mind, she thought she had a point. Our fees WERE double and the valuation WAS £60,000 less.

Hard for her to reconcile right...

But her place at that time was never worth £485,000.

It was worth £425,000

ut I had to be blunt and softly said, "I don't say things that sound nice to win instructions. **I care about outcomes** and don't fear my boss on Monday morning if I'm not instructed."

Sounds harsh, but my mission in this industry is to protect as many homeowners as I can from charlatans selling unrealistic dreams and snake oil...

In the end, we sold her home for £395,000

A £90,000 difference and £30,000 less than the £425,000 she should have got.

Now here is the thing.

The higher an agent's valuation is and the cheaper their fee's, i.e., the wider the gap, the more they're bullsh*tting you and the less likely they believe in their systems and or processes (if they have any).

The lower an agent's valuation compared to other agent's valuations and the higher their fee the more likely their results are far better.

In other words,...

Honesty is a very expensive gift.

Don't expect it from cheap agents...

STEP 8 - "BUYERS DON'T WANT CHEAP. BUYERS WANT BARGAINS..."

A surveyor following my TikTok channel gave away the exact formula to achieving the highest net profit when he wrote.

"Market low. Get lots of interest. Make buyers compete. The End."

When selling your home, the above is the exact script that will produce the highest net result for your home.

I've said it before, and I'll say it again.

Selling houses is the easiest thing in the world

But... and there's a big BUT...

To be successful as a seller, you have to understand the number one rule when it comes to selling homes...

"BUYERS DON'T WANT CHEAP. BUYERS WANT BARGAINS..."

Take 93 West Row in W10 below...

It's an ex-local authority flat I marketed for £349,950.

It took 60 days to go under offer and there were two offers neither of which wanted to go above £330,000.

We eventually sold for £334,000. Not great right.

Now compare that to the property below in W11 which is less than half a mile down the road.

So learning from my previous mistake with West Row, I marketed this 7th floor ex local authority flat in Lowerwood Court for £325,000

And sold it for £15,000 more than the asking price and crucially, £6000 more than West Row...

Why? Because buyers don't want cheap. Buyers want bargains...

And the above bargain took just 8 days to sell.

The difference between both sales.

Buyers for West Row stayed away making it look cheap because it just sat there online...

...and the lower priced property for Lowerwood Ct achieved multiple offers from buyers who couldn't afford to miss out on a bargain...

In other words, what looked cheaper achieved more because it looked like a bargain buyers couldn't put down.

STEP 9 - "AT THE END OF THE SALE, ALL THAT MATTERS IS YOUR PROFIT..."

Remember, **"IT'S NOT THE PROMISE OF PRICE THAT ACHIEVES THE HIGHEST NET PROFIT. IT'S THE PROCESS THAT ACHIEVES THE HIGHEST NET PROFIT..."**

Couple that with what the surveyor said, **"Market low. Get lots of interest. Make them compete..."** it really is the formula to successfully achieving the highest net profit for your property.

And the most important thing in the world that this formula will give you that unprofessional, unskilled, and unethical agents will never offer you...

--> CHOICE <--

- Choice to choose from the best buyers.
- Choice to choose what he next chapter in your life looks like.
- Choice of being in control the timescales

For example.

Achieving the highest net profit, is less about who offers you the most.

But the buyer who has the financial ability to proceed including the ability to be flexible enough to go as fast or slow as you need them to.

In other words…

To achieve the highest net profit for your home is more about the buyer that can match themselves to what you want to happen in the next chapter of your life.

And only when seller's market their property at the right level will they have choice.

Below is a list of the top 4 (but not limited to) types or buyer

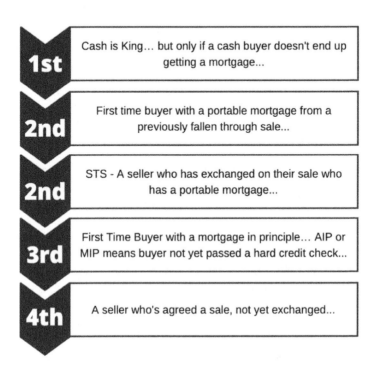

Remember what Rightmove said, "60% of sellers end up selling through the second agent..."

And the other 40% sell for an average of just 96% of an agent's suggested value.

I dread to think what the 60% eventually sold for.

The point I'm making.

If agents are honest, every property should sell for "100% of their marketed price FIRST TIME" unless that is, the seller pulls out...

If you want to be one of the 40% of sellers and sell for your asking price or more than the market value... market your property at or just below your property's provable value.

In a sea of overpriced properties, it'll look like a bargain giving you the choice of which buyer you'll sell your property to...

 aweakley
My house is on the market, got 35 viewings booked in on 2 open days. What happens if I can't find anything after it sells ? It will 100% sell v fast 1

The above comment is the utopia you want to when selling. Buyers falling over themselves to buy your property.

The mental thing in all of this.

If agents shared the same information I'm giving you now, their sellers wouldn't end up sinking to the bottom of the same stagnant pond of over-priced properties.

So make sure you don't lured into the promise of big money without massive evidence to support an agents claims.

Because you'll not just cost yourself thousands of pounds in lost ROI on the real value of your home...

You'll massively effect your choice to choose what happens next in your life.

"FINAL THOUGHTS..."

Here's the thing...

Before you go to market.

Before you even dare sign a contract.

You have to ask Estate Agents the questions highlighted in STEP 3 and be aware of the other steps.

The reason you're asking these questions is that you are trying to discover the difference between the professionals who deliver what they say they will versus the amateurs that just deliver words that sound nice...

All these questions are designed to deliberately attach a consequence to their actions.

Without consequences, agents will simply do what they want because no plan was ever put in place and you've signed a really long contract...

What are their self-imposed consequences?

The agent that says, **"If I don't deliver on the price point I've made you, I will sell your property for free..."** they're agent is taking maximum responsibility for their actions...

134

Said differently,

The agent that starts telling you a story of, "argh well you know…" and starts spinning you a yarn of "If, buts, maybe's, when's, whys," he or she has just told you the story of how they see the sale going at the price point they've just told you…

Remember your house sale is about you. About your journey. About the next chapter in your life

Not the agent's.

There are some fantastic agents out there.

Now you know what they look like :)

"WHAT NEXT...?"

Now you know the exact steps to achieve maximum profit when you sell your home...

How expert are you when it comes to what to look out for when it comes to buying your next property...?

You want the ultimate buyer guide?

Get your free download here → www.zerobsestateagency.com/ultimatebuyerguide and sign up to the daily Zero BS Estate Agency Newsletter...

Also, if you could help me get this book into as many sellers hands as possible by leaving a review on Amazon...

Even though I can't sell every sellers home, I believe every seller should have a copy this book in their hands before they go to market...

To your success…

Printed in Great Britain
by Amazon